FUN WITH NEXT TO NOTHING

Handicraft Projects for Boys and Girls

Written and illustrated by
WESLEY F. ARNOLD and WAYNE C. CARDY

SCHOLASTIC BOOK SERVICES
NEW YORK • TORONTO • LONDON • AUCKLAND • SYDNEY

Copyright © 1962 by Wesley F. Arnold and Wayne C. Cardy. This edition is published by Scholastic Book Services, a division of Scholastic Magazines, Inc., by arrangement with Harper & Row, Publishers, Inc.

5th printing .... March 1971

Printed in the U.S.A.

The "Boodle Box" and the Genie

What's a "Boodle Box"? Almost everyone has one. Many people have several. A Boodle Box is a box that holds all the odds and ends you have saved in case you might need them someday. It may contain anything from spools and buttons to Popsicle sticks and dented Ping-pong balls.

Call upon you imagination when you are making the projects suggested in this book! The things you can do are limitless. The fun you can have is unlimited, too.

The materials, steps to follow, and drawings will help you to get started, but summon up your genie to help you really go places.

You may not have a lamp with a genie inside, as Aladdin did, but your genie is probably in or around your Boodle Box.

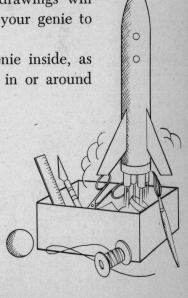

CONTENTS

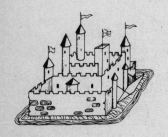 

Construction Hints

Papier-mâché

Sheet Method. Soak a sheet of newspaper in a thin mixture of paste. When it is soft and pliable, lay it over the form to be covered. Let dry.

Pulp Method. Tear newspaper into small pieces and soak these in water until they form a pulpy mass. Drain off the water and mix the paper thoroughly with thin paste. Apply by the handful to the form to be covered.

Strip Method. Tear off thin strips of newspaper and soak them in thin paste until they are soft and pliable. Apply in crisscross layers.

Salt-flour Mixture

Mix one cup of flour and one cup of salt. Add water carefully and stir until mixture is the thickness you desire.

Flour Paste

Mix one cup of flour and one teaspoon of salt. Add a very small amount of water and stir until mixture is like jelly. (A good commercial paste called wheat paste may be purchased at hardware or wallpaper-paint stores for very little money.)

Tempera Paints

Tempera paints are often called poster paints. For best results mix the paints with water until they are about as thin as light cream. If you are painting over a waxy surface (such as a milk carton), add a few drops of liquid detergent to your paint and it will cover better.

Ready-Set-Go!

There are some very important things you want to remember while you are making the projects shown in this book:

1. Get together all the materials you will need before you start.

2. If you can't find the exact material listed, think of a substitute.

3. Find a good place to work.

4. Safety first! If you are going to use a knife or shears, be extra careful. Don't forget to ask permission.

5. Before you start a project read the directions carefully and look at the drawings.

6. Don't be afraid to draw some of the things yourself rather than copy them.

7. Clean up! Find a good spot to keep your things while you are not working.

Now you are ready — get set — and go!

TRANSPORTATION

The story of how man learned to move across land and water is very interesting. The first wheel may have been a short log or a round stone with a hole at the center. Man's first boat probably was just a plain log. Later he improved on his first crude means of transportation and learned to use other and better materials. As time went on, man found more and more ways to travel faster and more comfortably.

You can make your own models of some of the things man has used for transportation over the centuries.

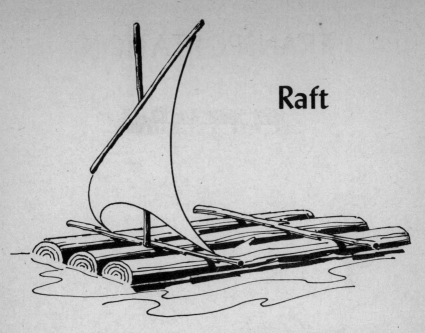

Raft

These are the materials you will need to make your model of a raft. Get all your materials together before you start your model:

> 5 or 6 straight branches, about 8 inches long
> 2 straight twigs, about the size of a pencil
> String

Here are the steps to follow in making your raft:

1. Cut all the branches to the same length.
2. Lay them side by side.
3. Bind the branches together and to the crosspieces with the string.

Canoe

These are the materials you need to make a canoe:

Heavy construction paper,   String
   light cardboard, or   Scissors
   real birchbark   Matchsticks
Darning needle   Crayons or paints

Follow these steps to make your canoe:

1. Fold the cardboard lengthwise lightly.
2. Cut the ends to the shape of a canoe.
3. Sew the ends together with an overhand stitch.
4. Insert matchsticks to hold the sides apart.

5. Decorate your canoe with Indian designs.

Suggested indian designs:

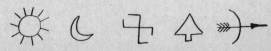

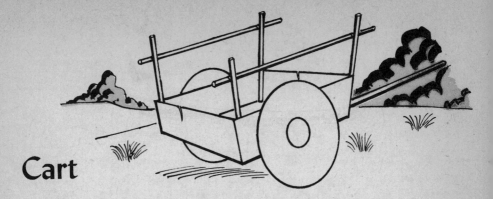

Cart

These are the materials you will need to make a cart:

Medium-sized cardboard box	7 round sticks
	Glue
2 pieces of light cardboard for wheels	Poster paint or crayons
	Scissors

These are the steps to follow in making a cart or wagon:

1. Use the cardboard box for the body of the cart.
2. Cut small circles from the light cardboard and pin or paste them on for the wheels.
3. Glue on a small round stick for the wagon tongue.
4. Glue the other sticks onto the box for side pieces.
5. Paint or color.

By making a few changes in the materials used and the steps to follow for the cart, you can make several different kinds of wagons.

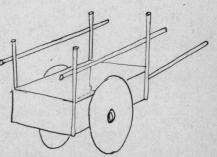

Covered Wagon

To make a covered wagon, use the same material as for the cart, except that you will need a longer, narrower box for the body and four wheels instead of two.

Other materials needed:

White paper for the top   Long stick for the wagon
Small matchbox for seat   tongue

These are the steps to follow in making a covered wagon:

1. Make the basic cart, using the four wheels.

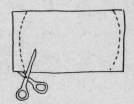

2. Glue the small matchbox on the front for the seat.

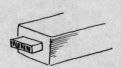

3. Cut a piece of white paper two inches longer than the box and three times as wide. Cut both ends of the paper so they curve outward.

4. Bend the paper and glue or paste the lower edges to the inside of the box to make the cover.

5. Glue the long stick on the front for the tongue.

Stagecoach

Here are the materials you will need to make a model of a stagecoach:

Square cardboard box
2 pieces of heavy
   cardboard a little larger
   than the box
4 pieces of heavy cardboard
   for the wheels
Paint

Long stick for the tongue
2 small boxes — one for
   the seat and one for the
   luggage carrier in the
   back
Glue

These are the steps to follow in making a stage-coach:

1. Draw the sides of the stagecoach on the two large pieces of heavy cardboard and cut them out.

2. Glue the sides to the box.
3. Glue on the small boxes for the seat and luggage carrier.

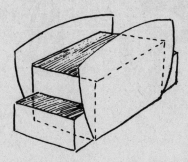

4. Cut out the wheels and glue them on.
5. Put on the tongue and paint or cut out doors and windows.
6. Decorate your stage-coach with paints or crayons.

Trains

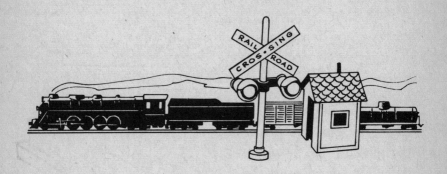

STEAM ENGINE

These are the materials you will need to make a steam engine:

Stiff cardboard for wheels
  and base
Small piece of light
  cardboard or tagboard
Piece of cardboard tube,
  between 2 and 2½ inches
  in diameter
Drinking straws

Matchbox or similar box
4 small spools
Paste or glue
Poster paint
Clippings from newspapers
  and magazines
  advertising railroads

Follow these steps to make the engine:

1. Cut the base for your engine from the stiff cardboard. It should be as long as you want your engine and as wide as a kitchen matchbox, plus one-inch flaps on each side.

2. Cut the end to a point and bend it down to form the cowcatcher. Bend the side flaps down to hold the wheels.

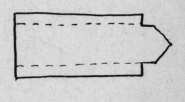

3. Cut the matchbox in half and glue one half on the end of the base for a cab. The open end of the matchbox half should face the rear.

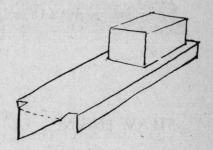

4. Cut a piece of cardboard tube to fit the base, for the boiler.

5. To cover the front end of the boiler, trace the end of the tube on a piece of light cardboard, cut out, and glue to the end.

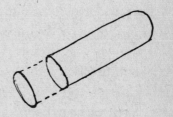

6. Glue the tube to the base and to the front of the cab.

7. Glue a small spool (lengthwise) on each side of the front end of the boiler and another one (on end) to the top, for a smokestack. Saw the fourth spool in half and glue the two halves to the top of the boiler behind the smokestack, as shown in the drawing.

8. Cut six big wheels and four small ones out of the stiff cardboard. Glue to the side flaps, as shown in the drawing.

9. Glue a straw on each side of the boiler for a side rail. Cut pieces of straws for the drive rods and glue them on the wheels, as shown in the picture.

10. Paint the engine black and decorate it with the clippings from the newspaper advertisements.

TOY TRAIN

Here is an interesting little train you can make for fun. These are the materials you will need:

Small round box for the boiler

Square boxes of various sizes

Spool

Long thin strip of cardboard

Small matchbox

Light cardboard for wheels and tops of cab and cars

Poster paints of bright colors

Paste or glue

Follow these steps to make your toy train:

1. Choose a large box for the cab and small round box for the boiler and paste them together to make the engine.

2. Glue on a spool for the smokestack.

3. Cut a flat piece of cardboard slightly larger than the cab and glue it to the top.

4. Glue on two large wheels in back, and two small wheels in front, cut from the light cardboard.

5. Use various-sized boxes for the different cars. For each box cut a flat piece of cardboard slightly larger than the top and glue it to the top for a roof.

6. Cut out two large wheels for each car and glue them in place.

7. For the caboose, make a car and glue the small matchbox to the top.

8. Paint and decorate your engine and cars.

9. When all the cars are finished and decorated, space them along the long strip of cardboard and glue them in place.

DE WITT CLINTON

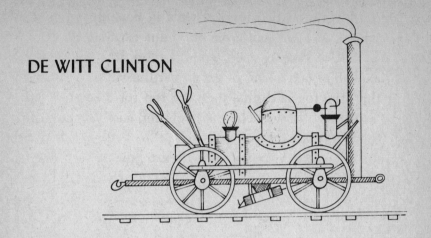

The DeWitt Clinton was one of the early trains in America. The steam engine had very large wheels and a tall smokestack. In 1831 this train made its first trip from Albany, New York, to Schenectady, New York. It took one hour and forty-five minutes to make the seventeen-mile trip in one direction.

People in those days thought the wood-burning train went very fast. It traveled almost thirty miles an hour.

You will need these materials to make a model of the DeWitt Clinton steam engine:

Round oatmeal box
    with lid
Lid of a shoebox
2 small spools
Light cardboard
Small square box, about
    half the size of a
    kitchen matchbox

2 cardboard tubes —
    one 8 inches,
    one 3 inches long
Paper fasteners
Large and small
    drinking straws
Glue (model airplane)
Paint

These are the steps to follow in making the DeWitt Clinton:

1. Glue the round box onto the cover of the shoebox.

2. Glue the long cardboard tube to the front of the round box. This will be the tall smokestack.

3. Glue the small square box to the back of the round box.

4. Carefully cut a hole in the center of the round box and insert the short piece of cardboard tube in the hole. Make a cover for this from light cardboard, and glue it on the top. This is the pressure dome.

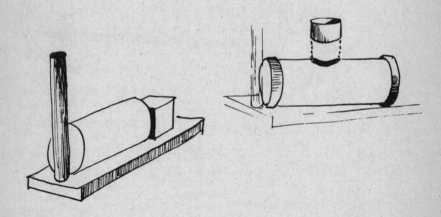

5. Cut four wheels four or five inches in diameter out of light cardboard. Draw spokes on each wheel.

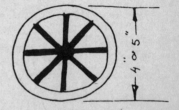

6. Fasten the wheels to the edge of the shoebox with paper fasteners.

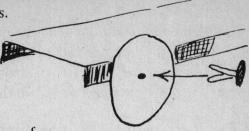

7. Glue a piece of a large drinking straw to the wheels 'on each side for driving rods.

8. Glue some short pieces of a small drinking straw to the side of the small square box. These are the throttle and control levers.

9. Glue the small spools to the top of the round box, one in front of and the other behind the pressure dome.

10. Paint your engine black.

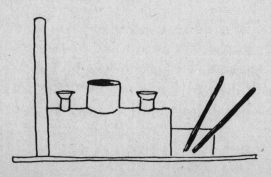

VIKINGS

The Vikings were daring sailors. They often traveled far from home. Often their trips were raids on the coasts of England and the mainland. The ships they used were long, with a carved head on the bow. Besides sails, they often carried oars. The Vikings hung their shields along the sides of the boat for protection.

You can easily make your own models of a Viking ship, a helmet, and a shield.

Viking Ship

Here are the materials you will need to build your own model of a Viking ship. Try to get all your materials together before you start building your model:

Piece of light cardboard about 12 inches long and 9 inches wide (such as laundries use to pack shirts) for the hull

A strip of light cardboard about 1½ inches wide, for model shields

Model airplane glue

7-by-8-inch piece of construction paper for the sail

Small flat sticks (Popsicle sticks or tongue depressors)

Small slender stick, about 10 inches long, for the mast

Needle

Black thread

Crayons

Small sticks for oars (lollipop sticks)

Flat (Popsicle) stick for the steering oar

These are the steps to follow in making your model:

1. Fold the piece of light cardboard the long way.
2. Draw an outline of a Viking ship. The bottom of the ship should be the fold in the cardboard.

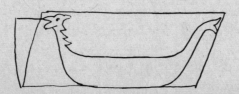

3. Keep the cardboard folded and cut out the ship. Do not cut along the bottom fold. Color the ship with crayons.

4. Sew the ends of the ship together with a needle and thread.

5. Cut three pieces of flat stick about two inches long. Place these in the top of the ship to hold the sides apart. Use a spot of glue to hold the sticks in place.

6. Make ten circles of cardboard one and a half inches in diameter for the shields. Draw Viking designs on the shields and color them with crayon. Glue five on each side of the ship.

7. Place the long slender stick for the mast against the forward crosspiece. Glue the lower end of the mast to the bottom of the boat. To make the mast stronger, glue it to the crosspiece also.

8. Cut the sail from colored construction paper in the shape shown in the drawing. With crayons make stripes or a design on the sail.

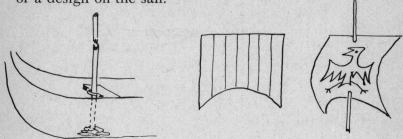

9. Punch holes in the sail and place it on the mast.

10. A small piece of ribbon may be attached to the top of the mast to serve as a pennant.

11. Punch some small holes between the shields. Insert the small sticks for oars. Glue a flat stick for a steering oar just behind the last shield.

Viking Helmet

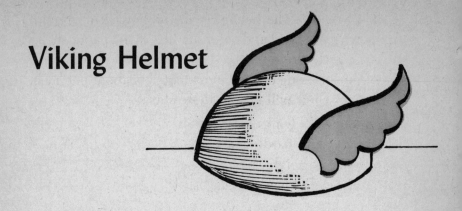

These are the materials you will need to make your Viking helmet:

Bowl or enamel pan,
   about the size of
   your hat
Strips of newspaper,
   about 1 inch wide
Light cardboard

Vaseline
Paste (poster, wallpaper,
   or flour paste, thinned
   with water)
Glue
Newspapers

These are the steps to follow:

1. Turn the bowl upside down on several layers of old newspapers and grease it well with Vaseline.

2. Soak the strips of newspaper in the thin paste. Lay them crisscross over the bowl until several layers have been built up.

3. Smooth off the surface with your fingers and let the paper strips dry for twenty-four hours.

4. To remove the helmet from the bowl, cut around the edge of the bowl and carefully lift off the paper shell.

5. Trim the edge neatly.

6. On each side of the helmet cut slits about one inch long. The wings will fit into these slits.

7. Make the wings out of the light cardboard. They can be six or eight inches long. Be sure to leave a tab at one end to slip into the slits on the sides of the helmet (see drawing). Color or paint the wings.

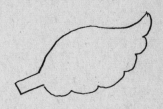

8. Fit the wings into the slits on the helmet and fasten them with a spot of glue on the inside.

9. Paint or color your helmet.

Viking Shields

The round shield was used by the Vikings for protection while fighting on land and also on the sea. The first shields were made by stretching layers of heavy skin over a frame of wood or bone. Each man decorated the shield with his own coat of arms or design.

To make a shield you will need these materials:

Cardboard (the side of a   Paint (poster or water
   cardboard carton)   color) or crayon
Paste or glue   Lightweight cardboard

Follow these steps in making your shield:

1. Cut out a large round piece of cardboard (eighteen to twenty-four inches across).

2. Draw a design on the cardboard and paint or color it.

3. Cut a round hole in the center of the shield.

4. Make a cone with a bottom edge larger than the hole in the shield. Cut several slits around the bottom edge.

5. Put the cone through the hole and fold the tabs down. Paste them flat.

6. Glue on the two cardboard handles to hold the shield on your arm.

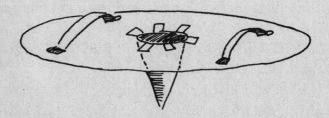

It is easy to make shields of your own designs. Use different shapes, sizes, and decorations.

EARLY MAN

One of the first shelters that early man had was the cave. The cave sheltered him from the weather and gave him some protection from animals and his enemies. Man was more comfortable and safer in his cave home than ever before. A fire at the entrance to the cave kept animals away and helped to keep him warm.

The cave men lived by hunting. They dressed in the skins of such animals as the mammoth, bear, and deer. They made their own weapons from stone. They chipped and polished stones into the shape of knives, axes, and spears, and fitted them with wooden handles.

Cave and Cave Men

These are the materials you will need to make a cave scene:

Newspapers
Small cardboard box,
    about 6 inches high
Poster paint or water
    colors
Paste
Large cardboard box
Brown wrapping paper
Small branches and twigs

Small stones and pebbles
Small piece of orange
    or red crepe paper
Plasticine
Small pieces of burlap
    sacking
Needle and thread
    or straight pins

These are the steps to follow:

1. Make your scene on the top of a table placed against the wall. Cover the table with heavy brown wrapping paper.

2. Cut off the top and one side of the large cardboard box and put it in the corner of the table near the wall. Color in sky and mountains, using paints or crayons.

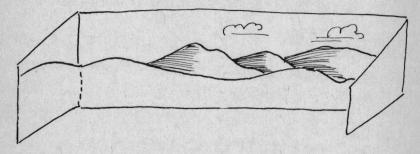

3. Cut a ragged hole in one side of the small cardboard box and place the box near the background.

4. Put wadded, dampened newspapers around the box to form the hills and uneven ground.

5. Wet some flat newspapers and lay them over the wadded papers. Pat them carefully to form the hills. When you are sure the newspapers are completely dry, paste down the loose edges and paint the ground and hills with poster paints or water colors.

6. Place some small stones around the mouth of the cave.

7. Use small branches for leafless trees. Stick twigs in the ground after carefully piercing holes for them with a sharp pencil point.

8. The fire is made from a small wad of red or orange crepe paper. Put this in front of the cave and pile twigs on top.

9. Model the cave people from plasticine. Remember to keep the size of the figures in proportion to the cave and the trees.

10. Burlap sacking is a very good material to use for clothing for the figures. You can sew the clothing on or keep it in place with pins stuck into the plasticine.

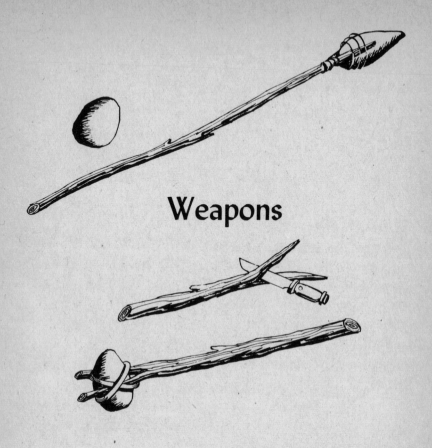

Weapons

Make weapons the right size for your cave men:

1. For an axe, split the end of a small green twig and bind a small pebble in the crack with thread.

2. Using a long stick and a pointed stone, make a spear the same way.

You can make larger weapons for display in the same manner.

SHELTERS

We know that early man lived in caves. Later he learned to do things with his hands and to build better shelters. Some were made of grass, reeds, and tree branches. Some were tents made from the skins of animals. Still later, man learned to make walls of logs and to use clay for plaster. As he learned to build, he also learned to use different materials.

You can make your own models of some of the shelters men in different parts of the world have used down through the ages.

Teepee

These are the materials you will need to make your model of a teepee:

Piece of brown craft or
    wrapping paper
    (12 by 12 inches)
Paste

6 straight twigs,
    about 8 inches long
Paints or crayons

These are the steps to follow in making your teepee:

1. Cut the paper into the shape shown in the picture.

2. Draw and paint on Indian designs.

3. Bring edges A and B together and paste.

4. Cut in a small door-way.

5. Put the sticks through the hole at the top of the teepee and paste or tape them to the inside.

Tent

Listed below are the materials you will need to make your model of a tent. Make your tent on a surface into which you can stickpins:

White cloth, 8 to 10 inches   Small paper flag
2 lollipop sticks for   Small stick, 8 inches long
   tent poles   for the ridgepole
6 straight pins

These are the steps to follow in making your tent:

1. Cut the cloth to the size given above.
2. Glue the ridgepole to the top of the tent poles.
3. Stand the lollipop-stick tent poles up and place the cloth over the ridgepole. Secure the two ten-inch sides of the cloth to the base with pins.

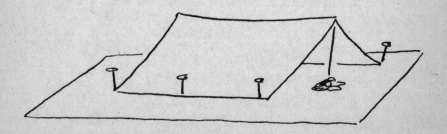

Log Cabin

There are two methods you can use to make your cabin: the twig method and the rolled-paper method.

TWIG METHOD

You will need these materials:

Straight twigs, pencil size
Cardboard box (the size you want to make your log cabin)

Glue
Piece of cardboard for the roof
Paint

These are the steps to follow in making your log cabin:

1. Cut the cardboard box to the shape shown here.

Cut out a door and windows.

2. Put a coat of glue on one side and lay the twigs on the glue. Put them close together to look like logs. Make sure your twigs are cut the right length. Do the same with the other sides.

3. Paint or color gray or black the piece of cardboard for the roof. Fold it and place it on the cabin.

ROLLED-PAPER METHOD

Here are the materials you will need:

Thin brown paper
Paste or glue
Piece of cardboard
   for the roof

Piece of cardboard
the size of the floor
of the cabin

You can use large drinking straws to build this cabin, or you can roll your own logs from the thin brown paper.

These are the steps to follow in making your log cabin:

1. To make the logs, roll a piece of the thin brown paper around a pencil, slide the pencil out, and paste the edge. Make enough logs for your cabin.

2. Glue the paper logs horizontally around the edges of the cardboard floor of the cabin. Then build them up, one on top of the other. Remember to leave openings for your door and windows.

3. Make the roof the same as for the cabin of twigs.

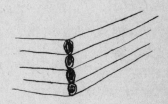

Adobe House

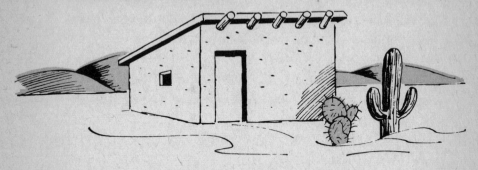

You will need these materials for your house:

Square box (the size you
   want to make your house)
6 or 8 straight twigs
   or sticks, about 2 inches
   longer than the box is
   wide
Glue
Salt

Piece of cardboard for
   the roof, about 1 inch
   longer and wider
   than the box
Flour
Water
Poster paint or water colors

These are the steps to follow in making your adobe house:

1. Turn the box upside down and cut in a door and window. Make the window small and square.

2. With a pencil, punch holes in the front of the box about one half inch from the top. Insert the twigs for the rafters and let the ends stick out about one inch.

3. Glue the cardboard roof to the top.

4. Mix a thin paste of flour, salt, and water. Add three tablespoons of salt to one tablespoon of flour, and then mix with water. Paint the entire adobe house with this paste.

5. When the paste is dry, paint the house with light-brown poster paint or water colors.

Grass Hut

Here is what you will need to make a grass hut:

Round oatmeal box or
   large cardboard tube
Cone-shaped drinking
   cup or ice-cream dish

Model airplane glue or
   rubber cement
Straw, dried grass,
   or hay

These are the steps to follow in making your grass hut:

1. Cut the round box down to the height you want your hut.

2. Turn the cone-shaped drinking cup upside down on the round box and glue it in place.

3. Cut in a small door.

4. Coat a small section of the side of the hut with glue or rubber cement, and while the glue is still wet lay on the straw or grass, until the area is completely covered. Continue to cover the sides — a small section at a time — in this way, and then do the roof.

Igloo

To make an igloo you will need these materials:

Bowl or round
    enamel pan
Strips of newspaper,
    about 1 inch wide
Paste (poster paste or
    flour thinned
    with water)

Vaseline
Glue
Newspaper
Small piece of thin
    white cardboard
Poster paint
Black crayon

These are the steps to follow in making your igloo:

1. Turn the bowl upside down on several layers of newspaper.
2. Grease the outside of the bowl with Vaseline.
3. Soak the strips of paper in thin paste and lay them crisscross over the bowl until several layers are built up.

4. Smooth off the surface with your fingers and let dry for twenty-four hours.
5. To remove the igloo shell from the bowl, cut around the edge of the bowl and lift the shell.
6. Cut out a round opening for the entrance tunnel.
7. Bend the piece of thin white cardboard, fit it into the opening, and glue it in place.

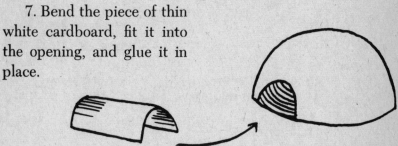

8. Paint the shell with white poster paint. When dry, draw on the snow blocks with black crayon.

ANCIENT ROME

In ancient times, many cities had to have aqueducts to get the water they needed. An aqueduct is a pipe or channel used to bring water to cities from distant places. The word *acqueduct* comes from two Latin words, one meaning "water" and the other "to lead."

The Romans built great stone troughs to get the water they needed. Sometimes the aqueducts had to cross valleys and streams. The Roman aqueducts were supported by stone arches, and these were often used to support roads as well as the water troughs.

The aqueducts of the ancient city of Rome were so well built that parts of them are still standing today.

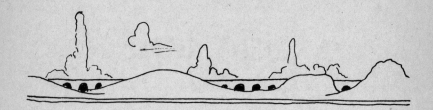

Roman Aqueduct

To make a Roman aqueduct and the surrounding scene, you will need these materials:

Large cardboard carton (the kind used to ship soap flakes or cereals)

Plasticine or modeling clay

Small box for house (ink-bottle box or matchbox)

Small piece of corrugated cardboard

Small matchbox for wagon

Light cardboard

Brown wrapping paper

Newspapers

Round toothpick

Paste

Straight pins

Small (lollipop) stick

Poster paint or water colors

Crayons

These are the steps to follow to make the aqueduct:

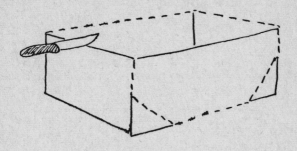

1. Cut off the top of the large box. Next, cut out the front, but leave the front corners.

2. Crumple some newspapers, dampen them slightly, and fill in the left and right corners with them.

3. Take more newspapers — double thickness — wet them, and lay them carefully over the crumpled papers. This will make the valley.

4. Paint the valley with a thin mixture of paste and water. Make sure all the edges of newspaper are stuck to the sides of the box.

5. When all the paste is dry, paint or color simple hills and trees and a blue sky on the sides and back of the box. Paint the newspaper hills. Green, brown, and tan are good colors to use.

6. You can build up the aqueduct with single bricks of clay or plasticine, or to mold it from plasticine and mark the bricks on it with the point of a pencil.

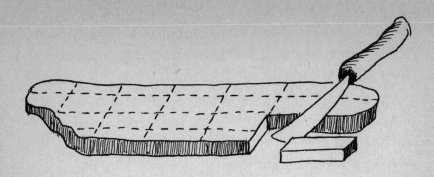

7. If you are going to build the aqueduct up from single bricks, the bricks can be made by the "pancake" method. Make a pancake of clay or plasticine, about a quarter-inch thick, on a flat surface. Use a paring knife to cut out individual bricks. Plasticine bricks of several different colors will look very nice.

Roman House

1. Cut the peak ends of the house from light cardboard and paste them on each end of a matchbox or ink-bottle box.

2. Fold a piece of corrugated cardboard for the roof. Paint this red, to make it look like tile. Paint on a small door and windows with black paint.

Wagon

1. The inside of a small matchbox will make the box of your wagon.

2. Cut out small circles from light cardboard and pin or glue them on for wheels.

3. To make the wagon tongue, glue on a round toothpick.

4. For the wagon cover, hoop a piece of brown wrapping paper over the top and paste it at each side.

Chariot

1. Draw the base or floor of your chariot on light cardboard and cut it out. Remember to leave tabs around the edge.

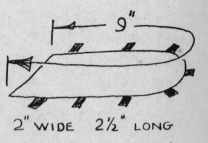

2" WIDE   2½" LONG

2. Draw the side and back panel of the chariot on light cardboard and cut it out. Carefully bend the panel and glue it to the folded-up tabs on the base.

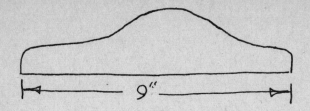

3. Cut small circles from light cardboard, and decorate them, for the wheels. Pin or paste them on the chariot.

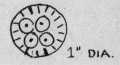

1" DIA.

4. Attach a small (lollipop) stick for the tongue.
5. Decorate the chariot with bright colors.

The animals to draw your wagon and chariot can be modeled from plasticine or cut from light cardboard. Toy animals can also be used.

CASTLE AND VILLAGE
OF MEDIEVAL TIMES

During the Middle Ages, many noblemen lived in large castles. These castles were really fortresses which protected the noblemen as well as the people who lived around him.

Castles were usually built in places that would make them hard to attack. They were often built on hills and surrounded by a moat, which was a wide ditch filled with water.

High, thick walls were built around the castle, with towers spaced among them. From these walls the nobleman and his soldiers could fight attacking enemies.

Inside the castle walls there were usually several small buildings, including the barracks for the soldiers, kitchen, barns, storehouses, and a chapel. The main tower was called the "keep."

These are the materials you will need to make a medieval castle and village:

Small boxes (for cigars, ink-bottles, matches)

Different kinds of round boxes or tubes (oatmeal boxes, cardboard tubes)

Cone-shaped paper cups

Plasticine or modeling clay

Small twigs and cotton balls to make trees

Thread or string

Straw, dried grass, or hay for roof

Poster paints or water colors

Crayons

Piece of sponge

Brown wrapping paper

Glue (model airplane or rubber cement)

Lightweight cardboard

If you wish to make your castle on a hilltop, follow the steps for making a hill outlined in the "Cave and Cave Man" or "Roman Aqueduct" project (see pages 33 and 50).

These are the steps to follow:

1. Before you start to build your castle and village, you will need to have an idea of where the different buildings and things will be placed. Cover the top of the table upon which you are going to build the castle and village with brown wrapping paper. Draw on the paper the general location of the castle, buildings, streams, moat, and roads.

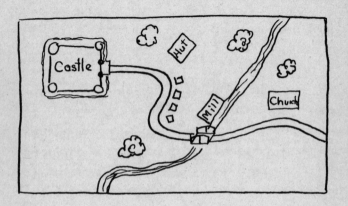

2. Put different-sized boxes together to form the castle. The boxes can be covered with construction paper or painted. Draw stones on with a black crayon. Color in or cut out the windows.

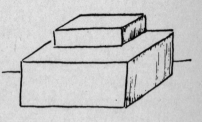

3. Castle walls can be built up from blocks of plasticine or clay, or made from strips of cardboard — with stones drawn on with crayon — set on edge and glued together.

4. Use cardboard tubes and round boxes for the towers. You can glue these to the walls or cut slits in them and slip them over the walls. Draw stones on with a black crayon. The pointed roofs of the towers are made by gluing on cone-shaped paper cups. The ramparts are notches cut into the top of the walls and larger towers.

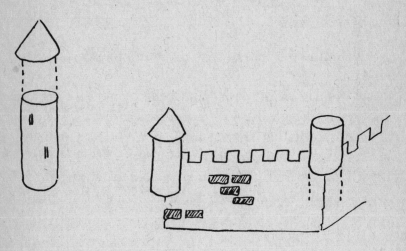

5. There should be a small tower on each side of the drawbridge. The drawbridge can be made of cardboard, hinging one edge with tape. The chains used to raise and lower the drawbridge can be made from string or thread.

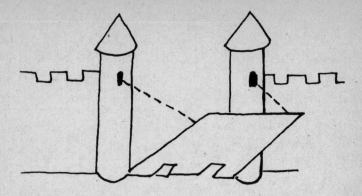

6. Paint in the water in the moat and the stream with blue paint.

7. Paint in roads, paths, and fields. Yellows, browns, and greens are good colors to use for these.

8. Make the hut from a small box. Glue on pointed ends made of light cardboard, and fold a piece of cardboard for the roof. Glue small pieces of straw, dried grass, or hay on the roof to make it look like a thatched roof.

9. Make the church the same way you made the hut, but add a steeple and paint the roof instead of covering it with straw.

10. The mill is placed at the edge of the stream. Build it the same as the hut. The water wheel can be made from plasticine or from the bottom of a round box or paper cup. Color or crayon in the spokes and rim.

11. To make the trees, form a wad of cotton on the end of a stick and pat it with a brush dipped in green paint. To hold these trees up, stick the end of the trunks into a piece of plasticine. Trees without leaves are made from branched twigs.

12. For the shrubs and bushes tear an old sponge into small ragged pieces. Dip the pieces into green poster paint.

13. A small stone wall can be built up along the road or between the fields with stones made from plasticine.

14. Make a small bridge over the stream with plasticine.

SPACE SHIPS AND MOON BASE

Down through the ages, man has dreamed of reaching worlds in outer space, and in recent years these dreams have begun to come true. Men have already made short journeys into space. Someday they will travel to distant moons and planets.

You can build a model ship of your own. Here are some suggestions.

Rocket Ships

To make model space ships, you will need these materials:

Cardboard tubes of
    various sizes
Cone-shaped paper cups
Light cardboard for fins

Drinking straws
Glue (model airplane)
Paint (poster or
    water color)

SINGLE-STAGE ROCKET

These are the steps to follow to make a single-stage rocket ship:

1. Select a cardboard tube the length and size you want your rocket ship to be.

2. Glue a cone-shaped paper cup on the front end. This is the nose of the rocket.

3. Cut four fins any shape you want.

4. Cut four slits near the back end of the tube, insert the fins, and glue them in place.

5. On each side of each fin glue a short piece of drinking straw to represent directional rockets.

6. Glue some short pieces of drinking straw to the inside of the rear end of the tube. These are the exhaust tubes of the powerful booster rockets that lift the ship off the ground.

7. Paint the rocket ship with bright colors. Paint or draw on the portholes.

MULTIPLE-STAGE ROCKET

If you wish to make a longer rocket ship, add additional stages. Each stage should be slightly larger than the one in front of it.

1. To make a two-stage rocket, choose two cardboard tubes, one slightly larger than the other.
2. Glue a cone-shaped paper cup to the front end of the larger tube and trim the edge of the cup even with the tube.
3. Insert the point of the cup into one end of the smaller tube and glue it in place.

4. Glue another cone-shaped cup to the other end of the smaller tube and trim the edge of the cup even with the tube.
5. Add cardboard fins and glue on pieces of drinking straws for the directional rockets and the booster exhaust tubes.
6. Paint and decorate the ship.

A Moon Base

Your rocket ship should have a base to blast off from as it starts its journey to another planet or moon. Let's imagine our base is located on a small moon in outer space. This moon has no air, no water, no forests. The base may be on a great level plain or in rough, steep mountains, with deep craters and other scars.

BASE AND BACKGROUND

To make the base and background, you will need these materials:

Large cardboard carton   **Poster paints**

These are the steps to follow to make your base and background:

1. Set up the carton so that one of the larger sides will form the bottom of your base. Cut off the top and two sides, leaving two connecting sides.

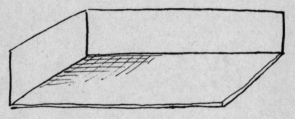

2. Paint on rough, jagged mountains and a sky. Make the sky dark blue or purple, and the mountains browns and yellows. Paint the base an earth or sand color.

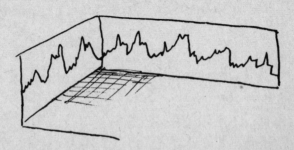

If you wish to make the base in three dimensions, with rough, mountainous ground, follow the procedure given in the "Cave and Cave Men" or "Roman Aqueduct" project (see page 33 and 50).

LAUNCHING PAD

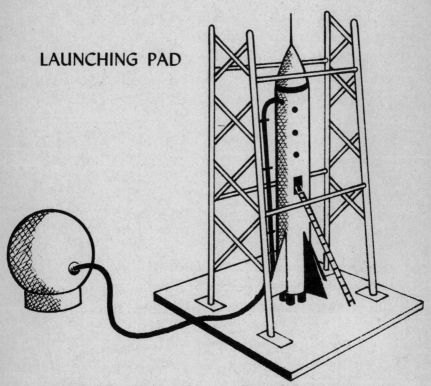

For the launching pad you will need these materials:

Sticks of various lengths
    or drinking straws
Toothpicks
Glue (model airplane)

Silver paint
Round shoestring with
    metal tip

Here are the steps to follow:

1. At the launch site, or pad, there will be metal uprights on each side of the rocket ship to hold it in position for launching. A long ladder will lead up to the door of the ship. The uprights will hold the fuel hose in place also.

2. Make your uprights and ladder by gluing sticks or straws and toothpicks together. Paint them with aluminum or silver paint to make them look like metal. The round shoestring will make your fuel line. If you wish, you can tape or glue this in place.

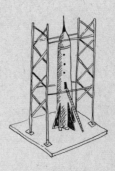

FUEL TANKS

For your fuel tanks you will need these materials:

Cardboard tubes of
    various sizes
Frozen-juice cans
Rubber ball the size of
    a tennis ball
Round thumbtack boxes
Drinking straws
Heavy cord

Toothpicks
Long thin sticks
Small cardboard boxes
    as bases for some of
    the tanks
Glue (model airplane)
Paint

Follow these steps to make your fuel tanks and lines:

1. The tanks will be of various sizes and shapes. The fuel lines, which are made of heavy cord and drinking straws, can be made to look like pipes or hoses. Some of the tanks will have ladders made from toothpicks glued to long thin sticks. Glue the hoses, pipes, and ladders in place, on and between the tanks. The drawings below will show you how to put the materials together.

2. Paint the parts that need painting so they will show up against the background.

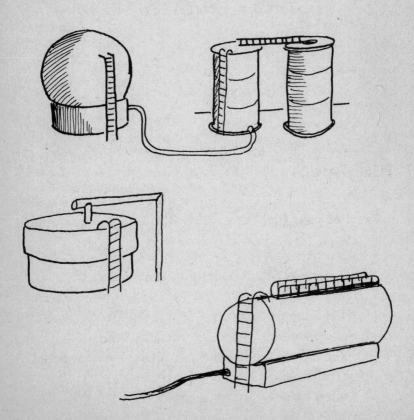

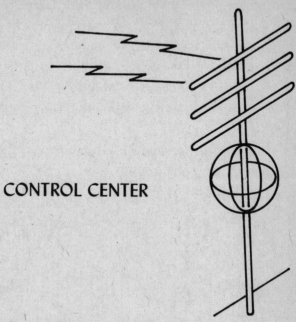

CONTROL CENTER

Here are the materials you will need:

Small boxes of various sizes   Toothpicks
Paint (poster and   Paper clips
    aluminum)   Ping-pong ball
Drinking straws   Glue

These are the steps to follow to make your control center:

1. Select several boxes of different sizes.
2. Paint boxes white, and paint doors and windows on them in black.
3. Group these buildings together.

4. Make radio and radar antennas by piercing drinking straws with toothpicks. Slip paper clips over a drinking straw for a TV antenna. Paint these aluminum. You can glue the antennas to the buildings or insert them in small holes punctured with a sharp pencil.

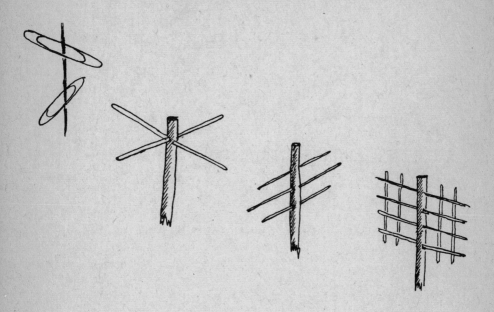

5. Make a radar or observation dome by cutting a Ping-pong ball in half and placing one half upside down on top of a building.

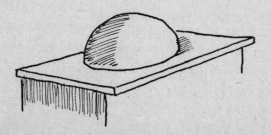

SPACE MEN

To make the space men, you will need these materials:

Plasticine or modeling   Straight pins
    clay (different colors)   Light cardboard
Toothpicks

Here are the steps to follow:

1. Make your space men with plasticine or clay of different colors, using a small lump to model the body and shoes. Use pins to hold the parts together and attach the men to the base of your station.

body shoes

2. The helmet is made of a small ball of modeling clay or plasticine with a small circle of light cardboard pinned to the helmet for a face plate.

helmet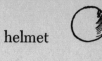

3. The control box is a small box made of plasticine or clay. A toothpick is inserted for the antenna.

SPACE WAGONS

These are the materials you will need:

Plasticine or modeling clay

Toothpicks

Straight pins

Light cardboard

Crayons

To make the space wagons, follow these steps:

1. Make the body of the wagon from modeling clay or plasticine. Make it about the size of a small match-box.

2. The control unit is a smaller square of modeling clay or plasticine placed on top of the body. Insert toothpicks for antennas.

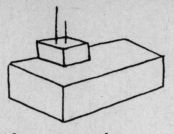

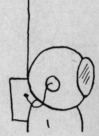

3. The driver is just the head and shoulders of a space man made with modeling clay or plasticine. Place the driver in front of the control unit.

3. Cut the tractor tracks from light cardboard. Draw in the treads with crayon, and pin the tracks to the body.

Space Helmet

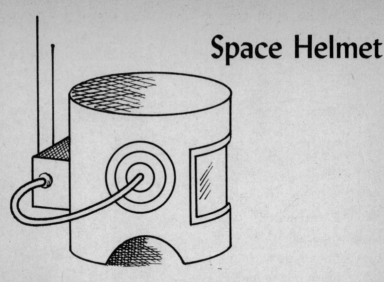

These are the materials needed to make a space helmet you can wear:

5-gallon ice-cream
    container (cardboard)
Piece of clear cellophane,
    about 6½ by 6½ inches
Glue
Stick 10 inches long,
    for antenna

Piece of cord
    24 inches long
Paint — silver and a dark
    color (blue or black)
2 paper fasteners
Large kitchen matchbox
Colored Scotch tape

Follow these steps in making your space helmet:

You can easily obtain an empty ice-cream carton or container from a restaurant or store. Wash it out well with cold water and let it dry.

1. Remove the metal band from the top of the container.

2. In the open end, cut out two pieces for your shoulders to fit.

3. Cut a hole about six inches square in the middle of the front.

4. From light cardboard, cut out two sets of discs for the earphones. Each set should have one disc about four inches across, one disc about three inches across, and one disc about two inches across.

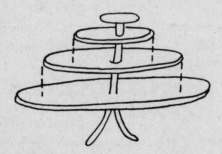

5. Fasten these discs together with a large brass paper fastener. Mount one set on each side of the helmet, using the paper fastener.

6. Glue a kitchen matchbox on the back for a radio. Glue a stick on the box for an antenna. Connect the earphones to the radio with short pieces of cord glued in place.

7. Fasten the cellophane face plate over the six-inch hole with a neat trim of colored Scotch tape.

8. Paint the helmet with silver paint and trim it with any dark color.

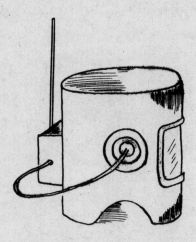

O papier mâché